**WOMEN'S PROFESSIONAL BASKETBALL**

# Teamwork:

# *The*

# HOUSTON COMETS

## in Action

**Thomas S. Owens**
**Diana Star Helmer**

The Rosen Publishing Group's
**PowerKids Press**™
New York

To everyone who has waited or worked for a dream. Here's proof that dreams come true.

Published in 1999 by The Rosen Publishing Group, Inc.
29 East 21st Street, New York, NY 10010

Copyright © 1999 by The Rosen Publishing Group, Inc.

First Edition

Book Design: Michael de Guzman

Photo Credits: pp. 4, 16 © Andrew D. Bernstein/WNBA Enterprises, LLC; pp. 5, 8, 12, © Bill Baptist/WNBA Enterprises, LLC; p. 7 © Reuters/John Kuntz/Archive Photos; p. 11 © Scott Cunningham, (inset) © Bill Baptist/WNBA Enterprises, LLC; p. 13 © Noren Trotman/ WNBA Enterprises, LLC; p. 15 © Glenn James/WNBA Enterprises, LLC; p. 19 © Nathaniel S. Butler/WNBA Enterprises, LLC; p. 20 © Andrew D. Bernstein, Brian Dear, Brett Coomer/WNBA Enterprises, LLC.

Owens, Tom,
    Teamwork: the Houston Comets in action / Thomas S. Owens, Diana Star Helmer.
       p.    cm. — (Women's professional basketball)
    Includes index.
    Summary: Profiles some of the key players on the Houston Comets and describes the team's first year in the WNBA.
    ISBN 0-8239-5246-0
    1. Houston Comets (Basketball team)—Juvenile literature. 2. Basketball for women—United States—Juvenile literature. [1. Houston Comets (Basketball team) 2. Women basketball players. 3. Basketball players.] I. Helmer, Diana Star, 1962-   . II. Title. III. Series: Owens, Tom, 1960-   Women's professional basketball.
    GV885.52.H68O94 1998
    796.323'64'097641411—dc21
                                                         98-17891
                                                          CIP
                                                           AC

Manufactured in the United States of America

# Contents

# First in Line

The Houston Comets had faced the New York Liberty three times and had lost each time. August 17 was Houston's last chance to beat New York. If they could do it, the Comets would be the first WNBA team good enough to play in the **championships** (CHAM-pee-un-ships).

Comets star Cynthia Cooper got just one basket in the first half. Then she got two more—and didn't stop. Tina Thompson and Tammy Jackson kept the ball from New York, getting twelve **rebounds** (REE-bowndz) each. The Comets finally beat New York, 70 to 55!

◀ The Comets worked their hardest to beat the Liberty.

5

# Sisters of the NBA

The idea for the WNBA began after the 1996 summer Olympics in Atlanta, Georgia. The whole world watched as the U.S. Women's Basketball Team won the gold medal. After the Olympics, the women's team traveled across America to meet fans. The American people wanted to be able to see these new basketball stars play in their own **league** (LEEG) in the United States.

As a result, the National Basketball Association (NBA) started the Women's National Basketball Association (WNBA). The women's teams would play in NBA team cities during the NBA's summer vacation. Houston fans were thrilled to find out that one of the first eight WNBA teams would be in their city.

The players on the U.S. Women's Olympic Team, such as Jennifer Azzi, were thrilled to win the gold. ▶

# Van Is Our Man

Van Chancellor was the only man to coach one of the first WNBA teams. Van had coached women's basketball for nineteen years. His college teams in Mississippi set records and won championships.

Houston was Van's first **professional** (proh-FEH-shuh-nul) team. He told them to work their hardest in the first five minutes of each half of the game. "If you can take care of the first five minutes," he said, "you don't have to worry about the last." Van was the WNBA's first Coach of the Year.

WNBA President Val Ackerman was happy to present the 1997 WNBA Coach of the Year Award to Van Chancellor.

# Oh, Baby!

College basketball star Sheryl Swoopes was the first female athlete to have a sport shoe named for her. In 1996, she shared Team USA's Olympic gold.

Four days after the WNBA season started, Sheryl had a baby boy! Six weeks later, she played in her first Comets game. "It's very important to me to show that it's possible to be a mom and an athlete," she said. Baby Jordan, who is named after basketball star Michael Jordan, travels with Swoopes. Her husband, Eric Jackson, is proud of what Sheryl is doing. He takes care of Jordan while Sheryl is making baskets.

Sheryl couldn't work too hard when she was pregnant with baby Jordan. But she worked extra hard after he was born. ▶

# Super Coop

For many years, the United States had no professional women's sports teams. Cynthia Cooper played for money and prizes in Italy. She was the top scorer there for eight years. She was tops when she joined the WNBA, too—in scoring, **assists** (uh-SISTS), and steals.

Sportswriters from all over the country voted Cynthia the WNBA's Most **Valuable** (VAL-yoo-bul) Player (MVP). But Cynthia says, "If it weren't for my team, I couldn't do anything out there." Cynthia's great playing helped cheer up her mom, who was sick. "My mom is my MVP," Cynthia says.

◀ The other WNBA teams expect Italy's top scorer to be tough so they play extra hard against Cynthia.

# Layups and Makeup

In college, Tina Thompson forgot to take off her lipstick before one of her games. She played so well in that game that she decided lipstick was lucky! She's played wearing lipstick ever since.

Tina was the very first player picked in the WNBA **draft** (DRAFT). "That was the highlight of my career," she says. Tina knows that she won't be a basketball player forever. During the WNBA off-season, Tina is studying to become a **sports lawyer** (SPORTZ LOY-yer). So even if she isn't on the court, her future plans still include basketball.

14

Tina Thompson was named to the All-WNBA First Team, an ▶ imaginary "dream team" of the league's best players.

# Knocked Out

With just eight minutes left in the **play-offs** (PLAY-offs), the Comets tied the Charlotte Sting. If Houston couldn't stay ahead in the game, they'd lose their chance at winning the championship.

"We wanted it so much that we were playing too hard," Tina Thompson said. Fighting for a rebound, Tina crashed into her teammate Wanda Guyton. They hit each other so hard that Wanda had to be carried off the court. That made the Comets play even harder. The players were strong and tough. They were tough enough to make it to the first WNBA championships.

◀ After running into teammate Tina Thompson, Wanda Guyton banged her head on the floor and had to be taken to the hospital.

# Last Chance

The Comets had just one game left—the championship. They were going to play against the New York Liberty, which was the only team that had beaten them three times. Worse, Wanda Guyton was hurt and couldn't play. "We need her," Coach Chancellor had said. But the rest of the team was ready to play. And they wanted to win.

Tammy Jackson played more than she'd ever played before. And she fought for every loose ball. New York stayed right behind Houston. Then, with nine minutes left, the Comets pulled ahead ten points. They didn't give up the lead again. The first WNBA championship trophy belonged to them!

18

The Houston Comets made history by winning the first WNBA championships. ▶

# Houston's Pride

The team's championship picture was on the front of cereal boxes sold in Houston. People in Houston paid money for the Comets' **autographs** (AW-toh-grafs). Coach Chancellor was very happy. He felt like he was dreaming. "I keep thinking that I am going to wake up," he joked. When the season began, the Houston Comets had lost four games and won only five. Coach Chancellor had said, "Those games told us what we could do, and what we couldn't." What they could do was have longer practices—up to three hours a day. "We worked hard," said Cynthia Cooper. And their work paid off!

◀ The Comets are happy to sign autographs and talk about basketball with their fans.

# Going Strong

No season would ever be like that first season for the Comets. There would be new teams to beat in the next year—in Washington, DC, and Detroit, Michigan. More games would be added to the season and the play-offs. Next year's semifinal and championship rounds would give teams more chances to win important games.

Many Comets, including MVP Cynthia Cooper, played professionally overseas during the off-season. They wanted to be ready for another WNBA year.

# Web Sites:

You can learn more about women's professional basketball at these Web sites:

http://www.wnba.com
http://www.fullcourt.com

22

# Glossary

**assist** (uh-SIST)  Passing to a teammate so she can score.

**autograph** (AW-toh-graf)  A famous person's signature.

**championship** (CHAM-pee-un-ship)  The last game of the season that determines which team is the best.

**draft** (DRAFT)  When teams take turns picking available players from college or other leagues to play on their team.

**league** (LEEG)  A group of teams who play against each other in the same sport.

**play-offs** (PLAY-offs)  Games played after the regular season has ended to see who will play in the championship game.

**professional** (proh-FEH-shuh-nul)  An athlete who gets payed to play a sport.

**rebound** (REE-bownd)  To get control of the ball after a missed shot.

**sports lawyer** (SPORTZ LOY-yer)  A person who knows the laws that teams and players should follow to be fair to each other.

**valuable** (VAL-yoo-bul)  Very important.

# Index